Little Duckling

Written by Alison Milford

Illustrated by Lucy Barnard

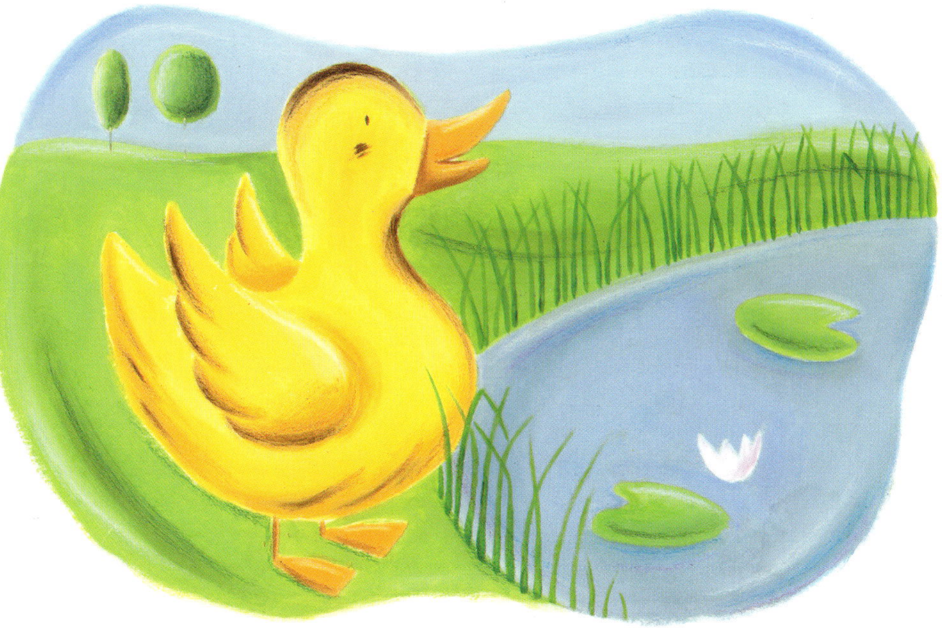

Little Duckling sees a rabbit.
"Will you play with me?"
says Little Duckling.

2

"Yes," says the rabbit.
"Come and hop with me."

The rabbit hops and hops.

"I can't hop with you," says Little Duckling.

Little Duckling sees a cat.
"Will you play with me?"
says Little Duckling.

"Yes," says the cat.

"Come and climb with me."

The cat climbs and climbs.

"I can't climb with you,"
says Little Duckling.

Little Duckling sees a dog.
"Will you play with me?"
says Little Duckling.

10

"Yes," says the dog.
"Come and run with me."

The dog runs and runs.

"I can't run with you,"
says Little Duckling.

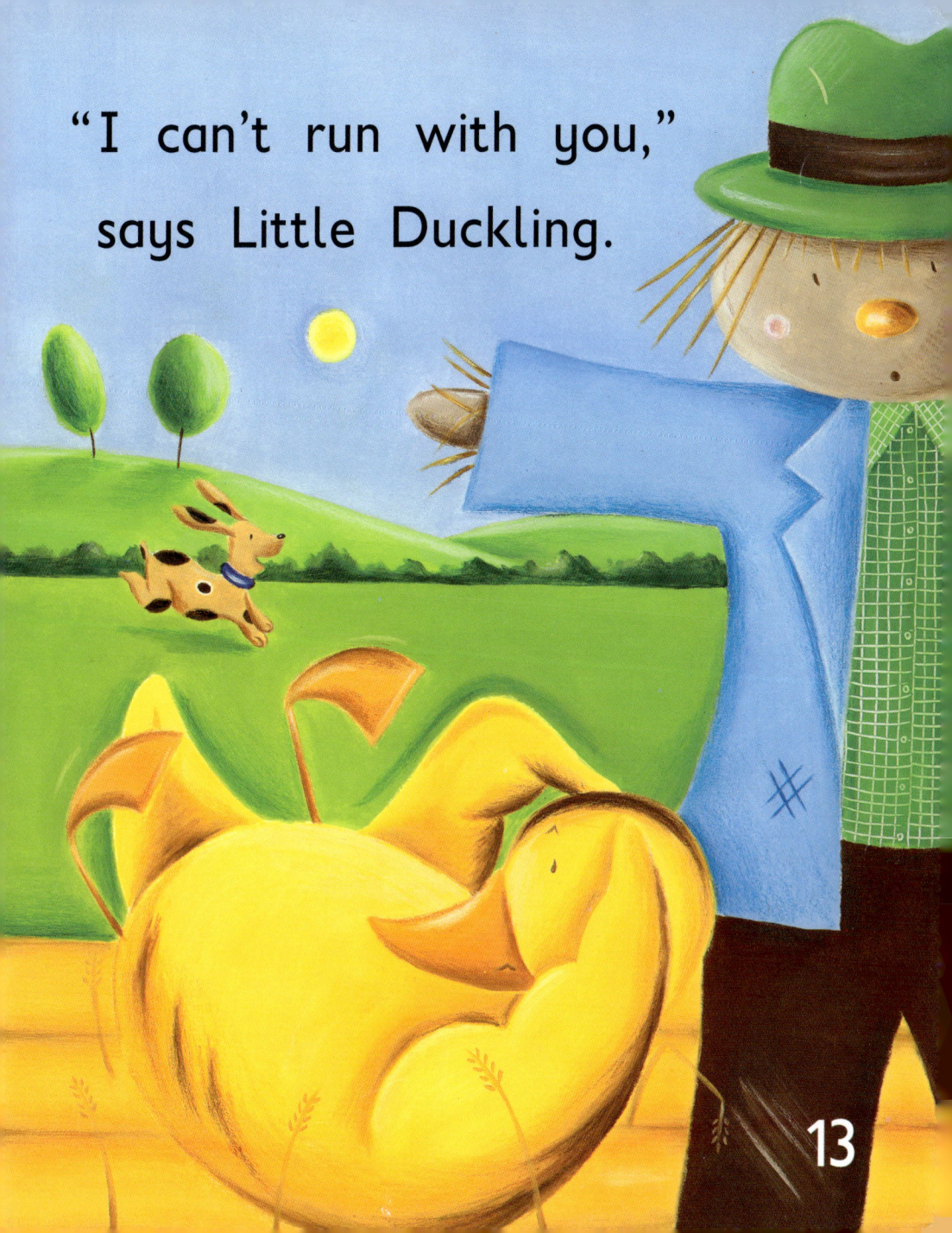

Little Duckling sees the ducks.
"Will you play with me?"
says Little Duckling.

"Yes," say the ducks.
"Come and swim with us."

"Look, I can swim with you," says Little Duckling!